Salomé
A Tragedy in One Act

Oscar Wilde

THE PERSONS OF THE PLAY

A YOUNG SYRIAN CAPTAIN

PAGE OF HERODIAS

FIRST SOLDIER

SECOND SOLDIER

CAPPADOCIAN

JOKANAAN

NAAMAN, THE EXECUTIONER

SALOMÉ.

SLAVE

HEROD

HERODIAS

TIGELLINUS

SLAVE

FIRST JEW

SECOND JEW

THIRD JEW

FOURTH JEW

FIFTH JEW

Scene—THE GREAT TERRACE OUTSIDE THE PALACE.

SCENE.

A great terrace in the Palace of Herod, set above the banqueting-hall. Some soldiers are leaning over the balcony. To the right there is a gigantic staircase, to the left, at the back, an old cistern surrounded by a wall of green bronze. Moonlight.

THE YOUNG SYRIAN

How beautiful is the Princess Salomé to-night!

THE PAGE OF HERODIAS

Look at the moon! How strange the moon seems! She is like a woman rising from a tomb. She is like a dead woman. You would fancy she was looking for dead things.

THE YOUNG SYRIAN

She has a strange look. She is like a little princess who wears a yellow veil, and whose feet are of silver. She is like a princess who has little white doves for feet. You would fancy she was dancing.

THE PAGE OF HERODIAS

She is like a woman who is dead. She moves very slowly.

[Noise in the banqueting-hall.]

FIRST SOLDIER

What an uproar! Who are those wild beasts howling?

SECOND SOLDIER

The Jews. They are always like that. They are disputing about their religion.

FIRST SOLDIER

Why do they dispute about their religion?

SECOND SOLDIER

I cannot tell. They are always doing it. The Pharisees, for instance, say that there are angels, and the Sadducees declare that angels do not exist.

FIRST SOLDIER

I think it is ridiculous to dispute about such things.

THE YOUNG SYRIAN

How beautiful is the Princess Salomé to-night!

THE PAGE OF HERODIAS

You are always looking at her. You look at her too much. It is dangerous to look at people in such fashion. Something terrible may happen.

THE YOUNG SYRIAN

She is very beautiful to-night.

FIRST SOLDIER

The Tetrarch has a sombre look.

SECOND SOLDIER

Yes; he has a sombre look.

FIRST SOLDIER

He is looking at something.

SECOND SOLDIER

He is looking at some one.

FIRST SOLDIER

At whom is he looking?

SECOND SOLDIER

I cannot tell.

THE YOUNG SYRIAN

How pale the Princess is! Never have I seen her so pale. She is like the shadow of a white rose in a mirror of silver.

THE PAGE OF HERODIAS

You must not look at her. You look too much at her.

FIRST SOLDIER

Herodias has filled the cup of the Tetrarch.

THE CAPPADOCIAN

Is that the Queen Herodias, she who wears a black mitre sewn with pearls, and whose hair is powdered with blue dust?

FIRST SOLDIER

Yes; that is Herodias, the Tetrarch's wife.

SECOND SOLDIER

The Tetrarch is very fond of wine. He has wine of three sorts. One which is brought from the Island of Samothrace, and is purple like the cloak of Cæsar.

THE CAPPADOCIAN

I have never seen Cæsar.

SECOND SOLDIER

Another that comes from a town called Cyprus, and is yellow like gold.

THE CAPPADOCIAN

I love gold.

SECOND SOLDIER

And the third is a wine of Sicily. That wine is red like blood.

THE NUBIAN

The gods of my country are very fond of blood. Twice in the year we sacrifice to them young men and maidens; fifty young men and a hundred maidens. But it seems we never give them quite enough, for they are very harsh to us.

THE CAPPADOCIAN

In my country there are no gods left. The Romans have driven them out. There are some who say that they have hidden themselves in the mountains, but I do not believe it. Three nights I have been on the mountains seeking them everywhere. I did not find them. And at last I called them by their names, and they did not come. I think they are dead.

FIRST SOLDIER

The Jews worship a God that you cannot see.

THE CAPPADOCIAN

I cannot understand that.

FIRST SOLDIER

In fact, they only believe in things that you cannot see.

THE CAPPADOCIAN

That seems to me altogether ridiculous.

THE VOICE OF JOKANAAN

After me shall come another mightier than I. I am not worthy so much as to unloose the latchet of his shoes. When he cometh, the solitary places shall be glad. They shall blossom like the lily. The eyes of the blind shall see the day, and the ears of the deaf shall be opened. The new-born child shall put his hand upon the dragon's lair, he shall lead the lions by their manes.

SECOND SOLDIER

Make him be silent. He is always saying ridiculous things.

FIRST SOLDIER

No, no. He is a holy man. He is very gentle, too. Every day, when I give him to eat he thanks me.

THE CAPPADOCIAN

Who is he?

FIRST SOLDIER

A prophet.

THE CAPPADOCIAN

What is his name?

FIRST SOLDIER

Jokanaan.

THE CAPPADOCIAN

Whence comes he?

FIRST SOLDIER

From the desert, where he fed on locusts and wild honey. He was clothed in camel's hair, and round his loins he had a leathern belt. He was very terrible to look upon. A great multitude used to follow him. He even had disciples.

THE CAPPADOCIAN

What is he talking of?

FIRST SOLDIER

We can never tell. Sometimes he says terrible things, but it is impossible to understand what he says.

THE CAPPADOCIAN

May one see him?

FIRST SOLDIER

No. The Tetrarch has forbidden it.

THE YOUNG SYRIAN

The Princess has hidden her face behind her fan! Her little white hands are fluttering like doves that fly to their dove-cots. They are like white butterflies. They are just like white butterflies.

THE PAGE OF HERODIAS

What is that to you? Why do you look at her? You must not look at her.... Something terrible may happen.

THE CAPPADOCIAN

[Pointing to the cistern.]

What a strange prison!

SECOND SOLDIER

It is an old cistern.

THE CAPPADOCIAN

An old cistern! It must be very unhealthy.

SECOND SOLDIER

Oh no! For instance, the Tetrarch's brother, his elder brother, the first husband of Herodias the Queen, was imprisoned there for twelve years. It did not kill him. At the end of the twelve years he had to be strangled.

THE CAPPADOCIAN

Strangled? Who dared to do that?

SECOND SOLDIER

[Pointing to the Executioner, a huge Negro.]

That man yonder, Naaman.

THE CAPPADOCIAN

He was not afraid?

SECOND SOLDIER

Oh no! The Tetrarch sent him the ring.

THE CAPPADOCIAN

What ring?

SECOND SOLDIER

The death-ring. So he was not afraid.

THE CAPPADOCIAN

Yet it is a terrible thing to strangle a king.

FIRST SOLDIER

Why? Kings have but one neck, like other folk.

THE CAPPADOCIAN

I think it terrible.

THE YOUNG SYRIAN

The Princess rises! She is leaving the table! She looks very troubled. Ah, she is coming this way. Yes, she is coming towards us. How pale she is! Never have I seen her so pale.

THE PAGE OF HERODIAS

Do not look at her. I pray you not to look at her.

THE YOUNG SYRIAN

She is like a dove that has strayed.... She is like a narcissus trembling in the wind.... She is like a silver flower.

[Enter Salomé.]

SALOMÉ

I will not stay. I cannot stay. Why does the Tetrarch look at me all the while with his mole's eyes under his shaking eyelids? It is strange that the husband of my mother looks at me like that. I know not what it means. In truth, yes, I know it.

THE YOUNG SYRIAN

You have just left the feast, Princess?

SALOMÉ

How sweet the air is here! I can breathe here! Within there are Jews from Jerusalem who are tearing each other in pieces over their foolish ceremonies, and barbarians who drink and drink, and spill their wine on the pavement, and Greeks from Smyrna with painted eyes and painted cheeks, and frizzed hair curled in twisted coils, and silent, subtle Egyptians, with long nails of jade and russet cloaks, and Romans brutal and coarse, with their uncouth jargon. Ah! how I loathe the Romans! They are rough and common, and they give themselves the airs of noble lords.

THE YOUNG SYRIAN

Will you be seated, Princess?

THE PAGE OF HERODIAS

Why do you speak to her? Why do you look at her? Oh! something terrible will happen.

SALOMÉ

How good to see the moon! She is like a little piece of money, you would think she was a little silver flower. The moon is cold and chaste. I am sure she is a virgin, she has a virgin's beauty. Yes, she is a virgin. She has never defiled herself. She has never abandoned herself to men, like the other goddesses.

THE VOICE OF JOKANAAN

The Lord hath come. The son of man hath come. The centaurs have hidden themselves in the rivers, and the sirens have left the rivers, and are lying beneath the leaves of the forest.

SALOMÉ

Who was that who cried out?

SECOND SOLDIER

The prophet, Princess.

SALOMÉ

Ah, the prophet! He of whom the Tetrarch is afraid?

SECOND SOLDIER

We know nothing of that, Princess. It was the prophet Jokanaan who cried out.

THE YOUNG SYRIAN

Is it your pleasure that I bid them bring your litter, Princess? The night is fair in the garden.

SALOMÉ

He says terrible things about my mother, does he not?

SECOND SOLDIER

We never understand what he says, Princess.

SALOMÉ

Yes; he says terrible things about her.

[Enter a Slave.]

THE SLAVE

Princess, the Tetrarch prays you to return to the feast.

SALOMÉ

I will not go back.

THE YOUNG SYRIAN

Pardon me, Princess, but if you do not return some misfortune may happen.

SALOMÉ

Is he an old man, this prophet?

THE YOUNG SYRIAN

Princess, it were better to return. Suffer me to lead you in.

SALOMÉ

This prophet ... is he an old man?

FIRST SOLDIER

No, Princess, he is quite a young man.

SECOND SOLDIER

You cannot be sure. There are those who say he is Elias.

SALOMÉ

Who is Elias?

SECOND SOLDIER

A very ancient prophet of this country, Princess.

THE SLAVE

What answer may I give the Tetrarch from the Princess?

THE VOICE OF JOKANAAN

Rejoice not thou, land of Palestine, because the rod of him who smote thee is broken. For from the seed of the serpent shall come forth a basilisk, and that which is born of it shall devour the birds.

SALOMÉ

What a strange voice! I would speak with him.

FIRST SOLDIER

I fear it is impossible, Princess. The Tetrarch does not wish any one to speak with him. He has even forbidden the high priest to speak with him.

SALOMÉ

I desire to speak with him.

FIRST SOLDIER

It is impossible, Princess.

SALOMÉ

I will speak with him.

THE YOUNG SYRIAN

Would it not be better to return to the banquet?

SALOMÉ

Bring forth this prophet.

[Exit the slave.]

FIRST SOLDIER

We dare not, Princess.

SALOMÉ

[Approaching the cistern and looking down into it.]

How black it is, down there! It must be terrible to be in so black a pit! It is like a tomb.... [To the soldiers.] Did you not hear me? Bring out the prophet. I wish to see him.

SECOND SOLDIER

Princess, I beg you do not require this of us.

SALOMÉ

You keep me waiting!

FIRST SOLDIER

Princess, our lives belong to you, but we cannot do what you have asked of us. And indeed, it is not of us that you should ask this thing.

SALOMÉ

[Looking at the young Syrian.]

Ah!

THE PAGE OF HERODIAS

Oh! what is going to happen? I am sure that some misfortune will happen.

SALOMÉ

[Going up to the young Syrian.]

You will do this tiling for me, will you not, Narraboth? You will do this thing for me. I have always been kind to you. You will do it for me. I would but look at this strange prophet. Men have talked so much of him. Often have I heard the Tetrarch talk of him. I think the Tetrarch is afraid of him. Are you, even you, also afraid of him, Narraboth?

THE YOUNG SYRIAN

I fear him not, Princess; there is no man I fear. But the Tetrarch has formally forbidden that any man should raise the cover of this well.

SALOMÉ

You will do this thing for me, Narraboth, and to-morrow when I pass in my litter beneath the gateway of the idol-sellers I will let fall for you a little flower, a little green flower.

THE YOUNG SYRIAN

Princess, I cannot, I cannot.

SALOMÉ

[Smiling.]

You will do this thing for me, Narraboth. You know that you will do this thing for me. And to-morrow when I pass in my litter by the bridge of the idol-buyers, I will look at you through the muslin veils, I will look at you, Narraboth, it may be I will smile at you. Look at me, Narraboth, look at me. Ah! you know that you will do what I ask of you. You know it well.... I know that you will do this thing.

THE YOUNG SYRIAN

[Signing to the third soldier.]

Let the prophet come forth.... The Princess Salomé desires to see him.

SALOMÉ

Ah!

THE PAGE OF HERODIAS

Oh! How strange the moon looks. You would think it was the hand of a dead woman who is seeking to cover herself with a shroud.

THE YOUNG SYRIAN

She has a strange look! She is like a little princess, whose eyes are eyes of amber. Through the clouds of muslin she is smiling like a little princess.

[The prophet comes out of the cistern. Salomé looks at him and steps slowly back.]

JOKANAAN

Where is he whose cup of abominations is now full? Where is he, who in a robe of silver shall one day die in the face of all the people? Bid him come forth, that he may hear the voice of him who hath cried in the waste places and in the houses of kings.

SALOMÉ

Of whom is he speaking?

THE YOUNG SYRIAN

You can never tell, Princess.

JOKANAAN

Where is she who having seen the images of men painted on the walls, the images of the Chaldeans limned in colours, gave herself up unto the lust of her eyes, and sent ambassadors into Chaldea?

SALOMÉ

It is of my mother that he speaks.

THE YOUNG SYRIAN

Oh, no, Princess.

SALOMÉ

Yes; it is of my mother that he speaks.

JOKANAAN

Where is she who gave herself unto the Captains of Assyria, who have baldricks on their loins, and tiaras of divers colours on their heads? Where is she who hath given herself to the young men of Egypt, who are clothed in fine linen and purple, whose shields are of gold, whose helmets are of silver, whose bodies are mighty? Bid her rise up from the bed of her abominations, from the bed of her incestuousness, that she may hear the words of him who prepareth the way of the Lord, that she may repent her of her iniquities. Though she will never repent, but will stick fast in her abominations; bid her come, for the fan of the Lord is in His hand.

SALOMÉ

But he is terrible, he is terrible!

THE YOUNG SYRIAN

Do not stay here, Princess, I beseech you.

SALOMÉ

It is his eyes above all that are terrible. They are like black holes burned by torches in a Tyrian tapestry. They are like black caverns where dragons dwell. They are like the black caverns of Egypt in which the dragons make their lairs. They are like black lakes troubled by fantastic moons.... Do you think he will speak again?

THE YOUNG SYRIAN

Do not stay here, Princess. I pray you do not stay here.

SALOMÉ

How wasted he is! He is like a thin ivory statue. He is like an image of silver. I am sure he is chaste as the moon is. He is like a moonbeam, like a shaft of silver. His flesh must be cool like ivory. I would look closer at him.

THE YOUNG SYRIAN

No, no, Princess.

SALOMÉ

I must look at him closer.

THE YOUNG SYRIAN

Princess! Princess!

JOKANAAN

Who is this woman who is looking at me? I will not have her look at me. Wherefore doth she look at me with her golden eyes, under her gilded eyelids? I know not who she is. I do not wish to know who she is. Bid her begone. It is not to her that I would speak.

SALOMÉ

I am Salomé, daughter of Herodias, Princess of Judæa.

JOKANAAN

Back! daughter of Babylon! Come not near the chosen of the Lord. Thy mother hath filled the earth with the wine of her iniquities, and the cry of her sins hath come up to the ears of God.

SALOMÉ

Speak again, Jokanaan. Thy voice is wine to me.

THE YOUNG SYRIAN

Princess! Princess! Princess!

SALOMÉ

Speak again! Speak again, Jokanaan, and tell me what I must do.

JOKANAAN

Daughter of Sodom, come not near me! But cover thy face with a veil, and scatter ashes upon thine head, and get thee to the desert and seek out the Son of Man.

SALOMÉ

Who is he, the Son of Man? Is he as beautiful as thou art, Jokanaan?

JOKANAAN

Get thee behind me! I hear in the palace the beating of the wings of the angel of death.

THE YOUNG SYRIAN

Princess, I beseech thee to go within.

JOKANAAN

Angel of the Lord God, what dost thou here with thy sword? Whom seekest thou in this foul palace? The day of him who shall die in a robe of silver has not yet come.

SALOMÉ

Jokanaan!

JOKANAAN

Who speaketh?

SALOMÉ

Jokanaan, I am amorous of thy body! Thy body is white like the lilies of a field that the mower hath never mowed. Thy body is white like the snows that lie on the mountains, like the snows that lie on the mountains of Judæa, and come down into the valleys. The roses in the garden of the Queen of Arabia are not so white as thy body. Neither the roses in the garden of the Queen of Arabia, the perfumed garden of spices of the Queen of Arabia, nor the feet of the dawn when they light on the leaves, nor the breast of the moon when she lies on the breast of the sea.... There is nothing in the world so white as thy body. Let me touch thy body.

JOKANAAN

Back! daughter of Babylon! By woman came evil into the world. Speak not to me. I will not listen to thee. I listen but to the voice of the Lord God.

SALOMÉ

Thy body is hideous. It is like the body of a leper. It is like a plastered wall where vipers have crawled; like a plastered wall where the scorpions have made their nest. It is like a whitened sepulchre full of loathsome things. It is horrible, thy body is horrible. It is of thy hair that I am enamoured, Jokanaan.

Thy hair is like clusters of grapes, like the clusters of black grapes that hang from the vine-trees of Edom in the land of the Edomites. Thy hair is like the cedars of Lebanon, like the great cedars of Lebanon that give their shade to the lions and to the robbers who would hide themselves by day. The long black nights, when the moon hides her face, when the stars are afraid, are not so black. The silence that dwells in the forest is not so black. There is nothing in the world so black as thy hair.... Let me touch thy hair.

JOKANAAN

Back, daughter of Sodom! Touch me not. Profane not the temple of the Lord God.

SALOMÉ

Thy hair is horrible. It is covered with mire and dust. It is like a crown of thorns which they have placed on thy forehead. It is like a knot of black serpents writhing round thy neck. I love not thy hair.... It is thy mouth that I desire, Jokanaan. Thy mouth is like a band of scarlet on a tower of ivory. It is like a pomegranate cut with a knife of ivory. The pomegranate-flowers that blossom in the gardens of Tyre, and are redder than roses, are not so red. The red blasts of trumpets that herald the approach of kings, and make afraid the enemy, are not so red. Thy mouth is redder than the feet of those who tread the wine in the wine-press. Thy mouth is redder than the feet of the doves who haunt the temples and are fed by the priests. It is redder than the feet of him who cometh from a forest where he hath slain a lion, and seen gilded tigers. Thy mouth is like a branch of coral that fishers have found in the twilight of the sea, the coral that they keep for the kings!... It is like the vermilion that the Moabites find in the mines of Moab, the vermilion that the kings take from them. It is like the bow of the King of the Persians, that is painted with vermilion, and is tipped with coral. There is nothing in the world so red as thy mouth.... Let me kiss thy mouth.

JOKANAAN

Never! daughter of Babylon! Daughter of Sodom! Never.

SALOMÉ

I will kiss thy mouth, Jokanaan. I will kiss thy mouth.

THE YOUNG SYRIAN

Princess, Princess, thou who art like a garden of myrrh, thou who art the dove of all doves, look not at this man, look not at him! Do not speak such words to him. I cannot suffer them.... Princess, Princess, do not speak these things.

SALOMÉ

I will kiss thy mouth, Jokanaan.

THE YOUNG SYRIAN

Ah! [He kills himself and falls between Salomé and Jokanaan.]

THE PAGE OF HERODIAS

The young Syrian has slain himself! The young captain has slain himself! He has slain himself who was my friend! I gave him a little box of perfumes and ear-rings wrought in silver, and now he has killed himself! Ah, did he not foretell that some misfortune would happen? I, too, foretold it, and it has happened. Well I knew that the moon was seeking a dead thing, but I knew not that it was he whom she sought. Ah! why did I not hide him from the moon? If I had hidden him in a cavern she would not have seen him.

FIRST SOLDIER

Princess, the young captain has just killed himself.

SALOMÉ

Let me kiss thy mouth, Jokanaan.

JOKANAAN

Art thou not afraid, daughter of Herodias? Did I not tell thee that I had heard in the palace the beatings of the wings of the angel of death, and hath he not come, the angel of death?

SALOMÉ

Let me kiss thy mouth.

JOKANAAN

Daughter of adultery, there is but one who can save thee, it is He of whom I spake. Go seek Him. He is in a boat on the sea of Galilee, and He talketh with His disciples. Kneel down on the shore of the sea, and call unto Him by His name. When He cometh to thee (and to all who call on Him He cometh), bow thyself at His feet and ask of Him the remission of thy sins.

SALOMÉ

Let me kiss thy mouth.

JOKANAAN

Cursed be thou! daughter of an incestuous mother, be thou accursed!

SALOMÉ

I will kiss thy mouth, Jokanaan.

JOKANAAN

I do no wish to look at thee. I will not look at thee, thou art accursed, Salomé, thou art accursed. [He goes down into the cistern.]

SALOMÉ

I will kiss thy mouth, Jokanaan; I will kiss thy mouth.

FIRST SOLDIER

We must bear away the body to another place. The Tetrarch does not care to see dead bodies, save the bodies of those whom he himself has slain.

THE PAGE OF HERODIAS

He was my brother, and nearer to me than a brother. I gave him a little box full of perfumes, and a ring of agate that he wore always on his hand. In the evening we used to walk by the river, among the almond trees, and he would tell me of the things of his country. He spake ever very low. The sound of his voice was like the sound of the flute, of a flute player. Also he much loved to gaze at himself in the river. I used to reproach him for that.

SECOND SOLDIER

You are right; we must hide the body. The Tetrarch must not see it.

FIRST SOLDIER

The Tetrarch will not come to this place. He never comes on the terrace. He is too much afraid of the prophet.

[Enter Herod, Herodias, and all the Court.]

HEROD

Where is Salomé? Where is the Princess? Why did she not return to the banquet as I commanded her? Ah! there she is!

HERODIAS

You must not look at her! You are always looking at her!

HEROD

The moon has a strange look to-night. Has she not a strange look? She is like a mad woman, a mad woman who is seeking everywhere for lovers. She is naked too. She is quite naked. The clouds are seeking to clothe her nakedness, but she will not let them. She shows herself naked in the sky. She reels through the clouds like a drunken woman.... I am sure she is looking for lovers. Does she not reel like a drunken woman? She is like a mad woman, is she not?

HERODIAS

No; the moon is like the moon, that is all. Let us go within.... You have nothing to do here.

HEROD

I will stay here! Manesseh, lay carpets there. Light torches, bring forth the ivory tables, and the tables of jasper. The air here is delicious. I will drink more wine with my guests. We must show all honours to the ambassadors of Cæsar.

HERODIAS

It is not because of them that you remain.

HEROD

Yes; the air is delicious. Come, Herodias, our guests await us. Ah! I have slipped! I have slipped in blood! It is an ill omen. It is a very evil omen. Wherefore is there blood here?... and this body, what does this body here? Think you I am like the King of Egypt, who gives no feast to his guests but that he shows them a corpse? Whose is it? I will not look on it.

FIRST SOLDIER

It is our captain, sire. He is the young Syrian whom you made captain only three days ago.

HEROD

I gave no order that he should be slain.

SECOND SOLDIER

He killed himself, sire.

HEROD

For what reason? I had made him captain.

SECOND SOLDIER

We do not know, sire. But he killed himself.

HEROD

That seems strange to me. I thought it was only the Roman philosophers who killed themselves. Is it not true, Tigellinus, that the philosophers at Rome kill themselves?

TIGELLINUS

There are some who kill themselves, sire. They are the Stoics. The Stoics are coarse people. They are ridiculous people. I myself regard them as being perfectly ridiculous.

HEROD

I also. It is ridiculous to kill oneself.

TIGELLINUS

Everybody at Rome laughs at them. The Emperor has written a satire against them. It is recited everywhere.

HEROD

Ah! he has written a satire against them? Cæsar is wonderful. He can do everything.... It is strange that the young Syrian has killed himself. I am sorry he has killed himself. I am very sorry; for he was fair to look upon. He was even very fair. He had very languorous eyes. I remember that I saw that he looked languorously at Salomé. Truly, I thought he looked too much at her.

HERODIAS

There are others who look at her too much.

HEROD

His father was a king. I drove him from his kingdom. And you made a slave of his mother, who was a queen, Herodias. So he was here as my guest, as it were, and for that reason I made him my captain. I am sorry he is dead. Ho! why have you left the body here? I will not look at it—away with it! [They take away the body.] It is cold here. There is a wind blowing. Is there not a wind blowing?

HERODIAS

No; there is no wind.

HEROD

I tell you there is a wind that blows.... And I hear in the air something that is like the beating of wings, like the beating of vast wings. Do you not hear it?

HERODIAS

I hear nothing.

HEROD

I hear it no longer. But I heard it. It was the blowing of the wind, no doubt. It has passed away. But no, I hear it again. Do you not hear it? It is just like the beating of wings.

HERODIAS

I tell you there is nothing. You are ill. Let us go within.

HEROD

I am not ill. It is your daughter who is sick. She has the mien of a sick person. Never have I seen her so pale.

HERODIAS

I have told you not to look at her.

HEROD

Pour me forth wine [wine is brought]. Salomé, come drink a little wine with me. I have here a wine that is exquisite. Cæsar himself sent it me. Dip into it thy little red lips, that I may drain the cup.

SALOMÉ

I am not thirsty, Tetrarch.

HEROD

You hear how she answers me, this daughter of yours?

HERODIAS

She does right. Why are you always gazing at her?

HEROD

Bring me ripe fruits [fruits are brought]. Salomé, come and eat fruit with me. I love to see in a fruit the mark of thy little teeth. Bite but a little of this fruit and then I will eat what is left.

SALOMÉ

I am not hungry, Tetrarch.

HEROD

[To Herodias.] You see how you have brought up this daughter of yours.

HERODIAS

My daughter and I come of a royal race. As for thee, thy father was a camel driver! He was also a robber!

HEROD

Thou liest!

HERODIAS

Thou knowest well that it is true.

HEROD

Salomé, come and sit next to me. I will give thee the throne of thy mother.

SALOMÉ

I am not tired, Tetrarch.

HERODIAS

You see what she thinks of you.

HEROD

Bring me—what is it that I desire? I forget. Ah! ah! I remember.

THE VOICE OF JOKANAAN

Lo! the time is come! That which I foretold has come to pass, saith the Lord God. Lo! the day of which I spoke.

HERODIAS

Bid him be silent. I will not listen to his voice. This man is for ever vomiting insults against me.

HEROD

He has said nothing against you. Besides, he is a very great prophet.

HERODIAS

I do not believe in prophets. Can a man tell what will come to pass? No man knows it. Moreover, he is for ever insulting me. But I think you are afraid of him.... I know well that you are afraid of him.

HEROD

I am not afraid of him. I am afraid of no man.

HERODIAS

I tell you, you are afraid of him. If you are not afraid of him why do you not deliver him to the Jews, who for these six months past have been clamouring for him?

A JEW

Truly, my lord, it were better to deliver him into our hands.

HEROD

Enough on this subject. I have already given you my answer. I will not deliver him into your hands. He is a holy man. He is a man who has seen God.

A JEW

That cannot be. There is no man who hath seen God since the prophet Elias. He is the last man who saw God. In these days God doth not show Himself. He hideth Himself. Therefore great evils have come upon the land.

ANOTHER JEW

Verily, no man knoweth if Elias the prophet did indeed see God. Peradventure it was but the shadow of God that he saw.

A THIRD JEW

God is at no time hidden. He showeth Himself at all times and in everything. God is in what is evil even as He is in what is good.

A FOURTH JEW

That must not be said. It is a very dangerous doctrine. It is a doctrine that cometh from the schools at Alexandria, where men teach the philosophy of the Greeks. And the Greeks are Gentiles: They are not even circumcised.

A FIFTH JEW

No one can tell how God worketh. His ways are very mysterious. It may be that the things which we call evil are good, and that the things which we call good are evil. There is no knowledge of any thing. We must needs submit to everything, for God is very strong. He breaketh in pieces the strong together with the weak, for He regardeth not any man.

FIRST JEW

Thou speaketh truly. God is terrible; He breaketh the strong and the weak as a man brays corn in a mortar. But this man hath never seen God. No man hath seen God since the prophet Elias.

HERODIAS

Make them be silent. They weary me.

HEROD

But I have heard it said that Jokanaan himself is your prophet Elias.

THE JEW

That cannot be. It is more than three hundred years since the days of the prophet Elias.

HEROD

There be some who say that this man is the prophet Elias.

A NAZARENE

I am sure that he is the prophet Elias.

THE JEW

Nay, but he is not the prophet Elias.

THE VOICE OF JOKANAAN

So the day is come, the day of the Lord, and I hear upon the mountains the feet of Him who shall be the Saviour of the world.

HEROD

What does that mean? The Saviour of the world.

TIGELLINUS

It is a title that Cæsar takes.

HEROD

But Cæsar is not coming into Judæa. Only yesterday I received letters from Rome. They contained nothing concerning this matter. And you, Tigellinus, who were at Rome during the winter, you heard nothing concerning this matter, did you?

TIGELLINUS

Sire, I heard nothing concerning the matter. I was explaining the title. It is one of Cæsar's titles.

HEROD

But Cæsar cannot come. He is too gouty. They say that his feet are like the feet of an elephant. Also there are reasons of State. He who leaves Rome loses Rome. He will not come. Howbeit, Cæsar is lord, he will come if he wishes. Nevertheless, I do not think he will come.

FIRST NAZARENE

It was not concerning Cæsar that the prophet spake these words, sire.

HEROD

Not of Cæsar?

FIRST NAZARENE

No, sire.

HEROD

Concerning whom then did he speak?

FIRST NAZARENE

Concerning Messias who has come.

A JEW

Messiah hath not come.

FIRST NAZARENE

He hath come, and everywhere He worketh miracles.

HERODIAS Ho! ho! miracles! I do not believe in miracles. I have seen too many. [To the page.] My fan!

FIRST NAZARENE

This man worketh true miracles. Thus, at a marriage which took place in a little town of Galilee, a town of some importance, He changed water into wine. Certain persons who were present related it to me. Also He healed two lepers that were seated before the Gate of Capernaum simply by touching them.

SECOND NAZARENE

Nay, it was blind men that he healed at Capernaum.

FIRST NAZARENE

Nay; they were lepers. But He hath healed blind people also, and He was seen on a mountain talking with angels.

A SADDUCEE

Angels do not exist.

A PHARISEE

Angels exist, but I do not believe that this Man has talked with them.

FIRST NAZARENE

He was seen by a great multitude of people talking with angels.

A SADDUCEE

Not with angels.

HERODIAS

How these men weary me! They are ridiculous! [To the page.] Well! my fan! [The page gives her the fan.] You have a dreamer's look; you must not dream. It is only sick people who dream. [She strikes the page with her fan.]

SECOND NAZARENE

There is also the miracle of the daughter of Jairus.

FIRST NAZARENE

Yes, that is sure. No man can gainsay it.

HERODIAS

These men are mad. They have looked too long on the moon. Command them to be silent.

HEROD

What is this miracle of the daughter of Jairus?

FIRST NAZARENE

The daughter of Jairus was dead. He raised her from the dead.

HEROD

He raises the dead?

FIRST NAZARENE

Yea, sire, He raiseth the dead.

HEROD

I do not wish Him to do that. I forbid Him to do that. I allow no man to raise the dead. This Man must be found and told that I forbid Him to raise the dead. Where is this Man at present?

SECOND NAZARENE

He is in every place, my lord, but it is hard to find Him.

FIRST NAZARENE

It is said that He is now in Samaria.

A JEW

It is easy to see that this is not Messias, if He is in Samaria. It is not to the Samaritans that Messias shall come. The Samaritans are accursed. They bring no offerings to the Temple.

SECOND NAZARENE

He left Samaria a few days since. I think that at the present moment He is in the neighbourhood of Jerusalem.

FIRST NAZARENE

No; He is not there. I have just come from Jerusalem. For two months they have had no tidings of Him.

HEROD

No matter! But let them find Him, and tell Him from me, I will not allow him to raise the dead! To change water into wine, to heal the lepers and the blind.... He may do these things if He will. I say nothing against these things. In truth I hold it a good deed to heal a leper. But I allow no man to raise the dead. It would be terrible if the dead came back.

THE VOICE OF JOKANAAN

Ah! the wanton! The harlot! Ah! the daughter of Babylon with her golden eyes and her gilded eyelids!—Thus saith the Lord God, Let there come up against her a multitude of men. Let the people take stones and stone her....

HERODIAS

Command him to be silent.

THE VOICE OF JOKANAAN

Let the war captains pierce her with their swords, let them crush her beneath their shields.

HERODIAS

Nay, but it is infamous.

THE VOICE OF JOKANAAN

It is thus that I will wipe out all wickedness from the earth, and that all women shall learn not to imitate her abominations.

HERODIAS

You hear what he says against me? You allow him to revile your wife?

HEROD

He did not speak your name.

HERODIAS

What does that matter? You know well that it is I whom he seeks to revile. And I am your wife, am I not?

HEROD

Of a truth, dear and noble Herodias, you are my wife, and before that you were the wife of my brother.

HERODIAS

It was you who tore me from his arms.

HEROD

Of a truth I was stronger.... But let us not talk of that matter. I do not desire to talk of it. It is the cause of the terrible words that the prophet has spoken.

Peradventure on account of it a misfortune will come. Let us not speak of this matter. Noble Herodias, we are not mindful of our guests. Fill thou my cup, my well-beloved. Fill with wine the great goblets of silver, and the great goblets of glass. I will drink to Cæsar. There are Romans here, we must drink to Cæsar.

ALL

Cæsar! Cæsar!

HEROD

Do you not see your daughter, how pale she is?

HERODIAS

What is it to you if she be pale or not?

HEROD

Never have I seen her so pale.

HERODIAS

You must not look at her.

THE VOICE OF JOKANAAN

In that day the sun shall become black like sackcloth of hair, and the moon shall become like blood, and the stars of the heavens shall fall upon the earth like ripe figs that fall from the fig-tree, and the kings of the earth shall be afraid.

HERODIAS

Ah! Ah! I should like to see that day of which he speaks, when the moon shall become like blood, and when the stars shall fall upon the earth like ripe figs. This prophet talks like a drunken man ... but I cannot suffer the sound of his voice. I hate his voice. Command him to be silent.

HEROD

I will not. I cannot understand what it is that he saith, but it may be an omen.

HERODIAS

I do not believe in omens. He speaks like a drunken man.

HEROD

It may be he is drunk with the wine of God.

HERODIAS

What wine is that, the wine of God? From what vineyards is it gathered? In what wine-press may one find it?

HEROD

[From this point he looks all the while at Salomé.]

Tigellinus, when you were at Rome of late, did the Emperor speak with you on the subject of...?

TIGELLINUS

On what subject, sire?

HEROD

On what subject? Ah! I asked you a question, did I not? I have forgotten what I would have asked you.

HERODIAS

You are looking again at my daughter. You must not look at her. I have already said so.

HEROD

You say nothing else.

HERODIAS

I say it again.

HEROD

And that restoration of the Temple about which they have talked so much, will anything be done? They say the veil of the Sanctuary has disappeared, do they not?

HERODIAS

It was thyself didst steal it. Thou speakest at random. I will not stay here. Let us go within.

HEROD

Dance for me, Salomé.

HERODIAS

I will not have her dance.

SALOMÉ

I have no desire to dance, Tetrarch.

HEROD

Salomé, daughter of Herodias, dance for me.

HERODIAS

Let her alone.

HEROD

I command thee to dance, Salomé.

SALOMÉ

I will not dance, Tetrarch.

HERODIAS

[Laughing].

You see how she obeys you.

HEROD

What is it to me whether she dance or not? It is naught to me. To-night I am happy, I am exceeding happy. Never have I been so happy.

FIRST SOLDIER

The Tetrarch has a sombre look. Has he not a sombre look?

SECOND SOLDIER

Yes, he has a sombre look.

HEROD

Wherefore should I not be happy? Cæsar, who is lord of the world, who is lord of all things, loves me well. He has just sent me most precious gifts. Also he has promised me to summon to Rome the King of Cappadocia, who is my enemy. It may be that at Rome he will crucify him, for he is able to do all things that he wishes. Verily, Cæsar is lord. Thus you see I have a right to be happy. Indeed, I am happy. I have never been so happy. There is nothing in the world that can mar my happiness.

THE VOICE OF JOKANAAN

He shall be seated on this throne. He shall be clothed in scarlet and purple. In his hand he shall bear a golden cup full of his blasphemies. And the angel of the Lord shall smite him. He shall be eaten of worms.

HERODIAS

You hear what he says about you. He says that you will be eaten of worms.

HEROD

It is not of me that he speaks. He speaks never against me. It is of the King of Cappadocia that he speaks; the King of Cappadocia, who is mine enemy. It is he who shall be eaten of worms. It is not I. Never has he spoken word against me, this prophet, save that I sinned in taking to wife the wife of my brother. It may be he is right. For, of a truth, you are sterile.

HERODIAS

I am sterile, I? You say that, you that are ever looking at my daughter, you that would have her dance for your pleasure? It is absurd to say that. I have borne a child. You have gotten no child, no, not even from one of your slaves. It is you who are sterile, not I.

HEROD

Peace, woman! I say that you are sterile. You have borne me no child, and the prophet says that our marriage is not a true marriage. He says that it is an incestuous marriage, a marriage that will bring evils.... I fear he is right; I am sure that he is right. But it is not the moment to speak of such things. I would be happy at this moment. Of a truth, I am happy. There is nothing I lack.

HERODIAS

I am glad you are of so fair a humour to-night. It is not your custom. But it is late. Let us go within. Do not forget that we hunt at sunrise. All honours must be shown to Cæsar's ambassadors, must they not?

SECOND SOLDIER

What a sombre look the Tetrarch wears.

FIRST SOLDIER

Yes, he wears a sombre look.

HEROD

Salomé, Salomé, dance for me. I pray thee dance for me. I am sad to-night. Yes; I am passing sad to-night. When I came hither I slipped in blood, which is an evil omen; and I heard, I am sure I heard in the air a beating of wings, a beating of giant wings. I cannot tell what they mean ... I am sad to-night. Therefore dance for me. Dance for me, Salomé, I beseech you. If you dance for me you may ask of me what you will, and I will give it you, even unto the half of my kingdom.

SALOMÉ

[Rising.] Will you indeed give me whatsoever I shall ask, Tetrarch?

HERODIAS

Do not dance, my daughter.

HEROD

Everything, even the half of my kingdom.

SALOMÉ

You swear it, Tetrarch?

HEROD

I swear it, Salomé.

HERODIAS

Do not dance, my daughter.

SALOMÉ

By what will you swear, Tetrarch?

HEROD

By my life, by my crown, by my gods. Whatsoever you desire I will give it you, even to the half of my kingdom, if you will but dance for me. O, Salomé, Salomé, dance for me!

SALOMÉ

You have sworn, Tetrarch.

HEROD

I have sworn, Salomé.

SALOMÉ

All this I ask, even the half of your kingdom.

HERODIAS

My daughter, do not dance.

HEROD

Even to the half of my kingdom. Thou wilt be passing fair as a queen, Salomé, if it please thee to ask for the half of my kingdom. Will she not be fair as a queen? Ah! it is cold here! There is an icy wind, and I hear ... wherefore do I hear in the air this beating of wings? Ah! one might fancy a bird, a huge black bird that hovers over the terrace. Why can I not see it, this bird? The beat of its wings is terrible. The breath of the wind of its wings is terrible. It is a chill wind. Nay, but it is not cold, it is hot. I am choking. Pour water on my hands. Give me snow to eat. Loosen my mantle. Quick! quick! loosen my mantle. Nay, but leave it. It is my garland that hurts me, my garland of roses.

The flowers are like fire. They have burned my forehead. [He tears the wreath from his head and throws it on the table.] Ah! I can breathe now. How red those petals are! They are like stains of blood on the cloth. That does not matter. You must not find symbols in everything you see. It makes life impossible. It were better to say that stains of blood are as lovely as rose petals. It were better far to say that.... But we will not speak of this. Now I am happy, I am passing happy. Have I not the right to be happy? Your daughter is going to dance for me. Will you not dance for me, Salomé? You have promised to dance for me.

HERODIAS

I will not have her dance.

SALOMÉ

I will dance for you, Tetrarch.

HEROD

You hear what your daughter says. She is going to dance for me. You do well to dance for me, Salomé. And when you have danced for me, forget not to ask of me whatsoever you wish. Whatsoever you wish I will give it you, even to the half of my kingdom. I have sworn it, have I not?

SALOMÉ

You have sworn it, Tetrarch.

HEROD

And I have never broken my word. I am not of those who break their oaths. I know not how to lie. I am the slave of my word, and my word is the word of a king. The King of Cappadocia always lies, but he is no true king. He is a coward. Also he owes me money that he will not repay. He has even insulted my ambassadors. He has spoken words that were wounding. But Cæsar will crucify him when he comes to Rome. I am sure that Cæsar will crucify him. And if not, yet will he die, being eaten of worms. The prophet has prophesied it. Well! wherefore dost thou tarry, Salomé?

SALOMÉ

I am awaiting until my slaves bring perfumes to me and the seven veils, and take off my sandals. [Slaves bring perfumes and the seven veils, and take off the sandals of Salomé.]

HEROD

Ah, you are going to dance with naked feet. 'Tis well!—'Tis well. Your little feet will be like white doves. They will be like little white flowers that dance upon the trees.... No, no, she is going to dance on blood. There is blood spilt on the ground. She must not dance on blood. It were an evil omen.

HERODIAS

What is it to you if she dance on blood? Thou hast waded deep enough therein....

HEROD

What is it to me? Ah! look at the moon! She has become red. She has become red as blood. Ah! the prophet prophesied truly. He prophesied that the moon would become red as blood. Did he not prophesy it? All of you heard him. And now the moon has become red as blood. Do ye not see it?

HERODIAS

Oh, yes, I see it well, and the stars are falling like ripe figs, are they not? and the sun is becoming black like sackcloth of hair, and the kings of the earth are afraid. That at least one can see. The prophet, for once in his life, was right, the kings of the earth are afraid.... Let us go within. You are sick. They will say at Rome that you are mad. Let us go within, I tell you.

THE VOICE OF JOKANAAN

Who is this who cometh from Edom, who is this who cometh from Bozra, whose raiment is dyed with purple, who shineth in the beauty of his garments, who walketh mighty in his greatness? Wherefore is thy raiment stained with scarlet?

HERODIAS

Let us go within. The voice of that man maddens me. I will not have my daughter dance while he is continually crying out. I will not have her dance while you look at her in this fashion. In a word, I will not have her dance.

HEROD

Do not rise, my wife, my queen, it will avail thee nothing. I will not go within till she hath danced. Dance, Salomé, dance for me.

HERODIAS

Do not dance, my daughter.

SALOMÉ

I am ready, Tetrarch.

[Salomé dances the dance of the seven veils.]

HEROD

Ah! wonderful! wonderful! You see that she has danced for me, your daughter. Come near, Salomé, come near, that I may give you your reward. Ah! I pay the dancers well. I will pay thee royally. I will give thee whatsoever thy soul desireth. What wouldst thou have? Speak.

SALOMÉ

[Kneeling].

I would that they presently bring me in a silver charger....

HEROD

[Laughing.]

In a silver charger? Surely yes, in a silver charger. She is charming, is she not? What is it you would have in a silver charger, O sweet and fair Salomé, you who are fairer than all the daughters of Judæa? What would you have them bring thee in a silver charger? Tell me. Whatsoever it may be, they shall give it you. My treasures belong to thee. What is it, Salomé?

SALOMÉ

[Rising].

The head of Jokanaan.

HERODIAS

Ah! that is well said, my daughter.

HEROD

No, no!

HERODIAS

That is well said, my daughter.

HEROD

No, no, Salomé. You do not ask me that. Do not listen to your mother's voice. She is ever giving you evil counsel. Do not heed her.

SALOMÉ

I do not heed my mother. It is for mine own pleasure that I ask the head of Jokanaan in a silver charger. You hath sworn, Herod. Forget not that you have sworn an oath.

HEROD

I know it. I have sworn by my gods. I know it well. But I pray you, Salomé, ask of me something else. Ask of me the half of my kingdom, and I will give it you. But ask not of me what you have asked.

SALOMÉ

I ask of you the head of Jokanaan.

HEROD

No, no, I do not wish it.

SALOMÉ

You have sworn, Herod.

HERODIAS

Yes, you have sworn. Everybody heard you. You swore it before everybody.

HEROD

Be silent! It is not to you I speak.

HERODIAS

My daughter has done well to ask the head of Jokanaan. He has covered me with insults. He has said monstrous things against me. One can see that she loves her mother well. Do not yield, my daughter. He has sworn, he has sworn.

HEROD

Be silent, speak not to me!... Come, Salomé, be reasonable. I have never been hard to you. I have ever loved you.... It may be that I have loved you too much. Therefore ask not this thing of me. This is a terrible thing, an awful thing to ask of me. Surely, I think thou art jesting. The head of a man that is cut from his body is ill to look upon, is it not? It is not meet that the eyes of a virgin should look upon such a thing. What pleasure could you have in it? None. No, no, it is not what you desire. Hearken to me. I have an emerald, a great round emerald, which Cæsar's minion sent me. If you look through this emerald you can see things which happen at a great distance. Cæsar himself carries such an emerald when he goes to the circus. But my emerald is larger. I know well that it is larger. It is the largest emerald in the whole world. You would like that, would you not? Ask it of me and I will give it you.

SALOMÉ

I demand the head of Jokanaan.

HEROD

You are not listening. You are not listening. Suffer me to speak, Salomé.

SALOMÉ

The head of Jokanaan.

HEROD

No, no, you would not have that. You say that to trouble me, because I have looked at you all this evening. It is true, I have looked at you all this evening. Your beauty troubled me. Your beauty has grievously troubled me, and I have looked at you too much. But I will look at you no more. Neither at things, nor at people should one look. Only in mirrors should one look, for mirrors do but show us masks. Oh! oh! bring wine! I thirst.... Salomé, Salomé, let us be friends. Come now!... Ah! what would I say? What was't? Ah! I remember!... Salomé—nay, but come nearer to me; I fear you will not hear me —Salomé, you know my white peacocks, my beautiful white peacocks, that walk in the garden between the myrtles and the tall cypress trees. Their beaks are gilded with gold, and the grains that they eat are gilded with gold also, and their feet are stained with purple. When they cry out the rain comes, and the moon shows herself in the heavens when they spread their tails. Two by two they walk between the cypress trees and the black myrtles, and each has a slave to tend it. Sometimes they fly across the trees, and anon they crouch in the grass, and round the lake. There are not in all the world birds so wonderful. There is no king in all the world who possesses such wonderful birds. I am sure that Cæsar himself has no birds so fair as my birds. I will give you fifty of my peacocks. They will follow you whithersoever you go, and in the midst of them you will be like the moon in the midst of a great white cloud.... I will give them all to you. I have but a hundred, and in the whole world there is no king who has peacocks like unto my peacocks. But I will give them all to you. Only you must loose me from my oath, and must not ask of me that which you have asked of me.

[He empties the cup of wine.]

SALOMÉ

Give me the head of Jokanaan.

HERODIAS

Well said, my daughter! As for you, you are ridiculous with your peacocks.

HEROD

Be silent! You cry out always; you cry out like a beast of prey. You must not. Your voice wearies me. Be silent, I say Salomé, think of what you are doing. This man comes perchance from God. He is a holy man. The finger of God has touched him. God has put into his mouth terrible words. In the palace as in the desert God is always with him.... At least it is possible. One does not know. It is possible that God is for him and with him. Furthermore, if he died some misfortune might happen to me. In any case, he said that the day he dies a misfortune will happen to some one. That could only be to me. Remember, I slipped in blood when I entered. Also, I heard a beating of wings in the air, a beating of mighty wings. These are very evil omens, and there were others. I am sure there were others though I did not see them. Well, Salomé, you do not wish a misfortune to happen to me? You do not wish that. Listen to me, then.

SALOMÉ

Give me the head of Jokanaan.

HEROD

Ah! you are not listening to me. Be calm. I—I am calm. I am quite calm. Listen. I have jewels hidden in this place—jewels that your mother even has never seen; jewels that are marvellous. I have a collar of pearls, set in four rows. They are like unto moons chained with rays of silver. They are like fifty moons caught in a golden net. On the ivory of her breast a queen has worn it. Thou shalt be as fair as a queen when thou wearest it. I have amethysts of two kinds, one that is black like wine, and one that is red like wine which has been coloured with water. I have topazes, yellow as are the eyes of tigers, and topazes that are pink as the eyes of a wood-pigeon, and green topazes that are as the eyes of cats. I have opals that burn always, with an icelike flame, opals that make sad men's minds, and are fearful of the shadows. I have onyxes like the eyeballs of a dead woman. I have moonstones that change when the moon changes, and are wan when they see the sun. I have sapphires big like eggs, and as blue as blue flowers. The sea wanders within them and the moon comes never to trouble the blue of their waves. I have chrysolites and beryls and chrysoprases and rubies. I have sardonyx and hyacinth stones, and stones of chalcedony, and I will give them all to you, all, and other things will I add to them. The King of the Indies has but even now sent me four fans fashioned from the feathers of parrots, and the King of Numidia a garment of ostrich feathers. I have a crystal, into which it is not lawful for a woman to look, nor may young men behold it until they have been beaten with rods. In a coffer of nacre I have three wondrous turquoises. He who wears them on his forehead can imagine things which are not, and he who carries them in his hand can make women sterile. These are great treasures above all price. They are treasures without price. But this is not all. In an ebony coffer I have two cups of amber, that are like apples of gold. If an enemy pour poison into these cups, they become like an apple of silver. In a coffer incrusted with amber I have sandals incrusted with glass. I have mantles that have been brought from the land of the Seres, and bracelets decked about with carbuncles and with jade that come from the city of Euphrates.... What desirest thou more than this, Salomé? Tell me the thing that thou desirest, and I will give it thee. All that thou askest I will give thee, save one thing. I will give thee all that is mine, save one life. I will give thee the mantle of the high priest. I will give thee the veil of the sanctuary.

THE JEWS

Oh! oh!

SALOMÉ

Give me the head of Jokanaan.

HEROD

[Sinking back in his seat]. Let her be given what she asks! Of a truth she is her mother's child! [The first Soldier approaches. Herodias draws from the hand of the Tetrarch the ring of death and gives it to the Soldier, who straightway bears it to the Executioner. The Executioner looks scared.] Who has taken my ring? There was a ring on my right hand. Who has drunk my wine? There was wine in my cup. It was full of wine. Someone has drunk it! Oh! surely some evil will befall some one. [The Executioner goes down into the cistern.] Ah! Wherefore did I give my oath? Kings ought never to pledge their word. If they keep it not, it is terrible, and if they keep it, it is terrible also.

HERODIAS

My daughter has done well.

HEROD

I am sure that some misfortune will happen.

SALOMÉ

[She leans over the cistern and listens.]

There is no sound. I hear nothing. Why does he not cry out, this man? Ah! if any man sought to kill me, I would cry out, I would struggle, I would not suffer.... Strike, strike, Naaman, strike, I tell you.... No, I hear nothing. There is a silence, a terrible silence. Ah! something has fallen upon the ground. I heard something fall. It is the sword of the headsman. He is afraid, this slave. He has let his sword fall. He dare not kill him. He is a coward, this slave! Let soldiers be sent. [She sees the Page of Herodias and addresses him.] Come hither, thou wert the friend of him who is dead, is it not so? Well, I tell thee, there are not dead men enough. Go to the soldiers and bid them go down and bring me the thing I ask, the thing the Tetrarch has promised me, the thing that is mine. [The Page recoils. She turns to the soldiers.] Hither, ye soldiers. Get ye down into this cistern and bring me the head of this man. [The Soldiers recoil.] Tetrarch, Tetrarch, command your soldiers that they bring me the head of Jokanaan.

[A huge black arm, the arm of the Executioner, comes forth from the cistern, bearing on a silver shield the head of Jokanaan. Salomé seizes it. Herod hides his face with his cloak. Herodias smiles and fans herself. The Nazarenes fall on their knees and begin to pray.]

Ah! thou wouldst not suffer me to kiss thy mouth, Jokanaan. Well! I will kiss it now. I will bite it with my teeth as one bites a ripe fruit. Yes, I will kiss thy mouth, Jokanaan. I said it; did I not say it? I said it. Ah! I will kiss it now.... But, wherefore dost thou not look at me, Jokanaan? Thine eyes that were so terrible, so full of rage and scorn, are shut now. Wherefore are they shut? Open thine eyes! Lift up thine eyelids, Jokanaan! Wherefore dost thou not look at me? Art thou afraid of me, Jokanaan, that thou wilt not look at me?... And thy tongue, that was like a red snake darting poison, it moves no more, it says nothing now, Jokanaan, that scarlet viper that spat its venom upon me. It is strange, is it not? How is it that the red viper stirs no longer?... Thou wouldst have none of me, Jokanaan. Thou didst reject me. Thou didst speak evil words against me. Thou didst treat me as a harlot, as a wanton, me, Salomé, daughter of Herodias, Princess of Judæa! Well, Jokanaan, I still live, but thou, thou art dead, and thy head belongs to me. I can do with it what I will. I can throw it to the dogs and to the birds of the air. That which the dogs leave, the birds of the air shall devour.... Ah, Jokanaan, Jokanaan, thou wert the only man that I have loved. All other men are hateful to me. But thou, thou wert beautiful! Thy body was a column of ivory set on a silver socket. It was a garden full of doves and of silver lilies. It was a tower of silver decked with shields of ivory. There was nothing in the world so white as thy body. There was nothing in the world so black as thy hair. In the whole world there was nothing so red as thy mouth. Thy voice was a censer that scattered strange perfumes, and when I looked on thee I heard a strange music. Ah! wherefore didst thou not look at me, Jokanaan? Behind thine hands and thy curses thou didst hide thy face. Thou didst put upon thine eyes the covering of him who would see his God. Well, thou hast seen thy God, Jokanaan, but me, me, thou didst never see. If thou hadst seen me thou wouldst have loved me. I, I saw thee, Jokanaan, and I loved thee. Oh, how I loved thee! I love thee yet, Jokanaan, I love thee only.... I am athirst for thy beauty; I am hungry for thy body; and neither wine nor fruits can appease my desire. What shall I do now, Jokanaan? Neither the floods nor the great waters can quench my passion. I was a princess, and thou didst scorn me. I was a virgin, and thou didst take my virginity from me. I was chaste, and thou didst fill my veins with fire.... Ah! ah! wherefore didst thou not look at me, Jokanaan? If thou hadst looked at me thou hadst loved me. Well I know that thou wouldst have loved me, and the mystery of love is greater than the mystery of death. Love only should one consider.

HEROD

She is monstrous, thy daughter, she is altogether monstrous. In truth, what she has done is a great crime. I am sure that it was a crime against an unknown God.

HERODIAS

I approve of what my daughter has done. And I will stay here now.

HEROD

[Rising].

Ah! There speaks the incestuous wife! Come! I will not stay here. Come, I tell thee. Surely some terrible thing will befall. Manasseh, Issachar, Ozias, put out the torches. I will not look at things, I will not suffer things to look at me. Put out the torches! Hide the moon! Hide the stars! Let us hide ourselves in our palace, Herodias. I begin to be afraid.

[The slaves put out the torches. The stars disappear. A great black cloud crosses the moon and conceals it completely. The stage becomes very dark. The Tetrarch begins to climb the staircase.]

THE VOICE OF SALOMÉ

Ah! I have kissed thy mouth, Jokanaan, I have kissed thy mouth. There was a bitter taste on thy lips. Was it the taste of blood?... But perchance it is the taste of love.... They say that love hath a bitter taste.... But what of that? what of that? I have kissed thy mouth, Jokanaan.

[A moonbeam falls on Salomé covering her with light.]

HEROD

[Turning round and seeing Salomé.]

Kill that woman!

[The soldiers rush forward and crush beneath their shields Salomé, daughter of Herodias, Princess of Judæa.]

CURTAIN.

www.ingramcontent.com/pod-product-compliance
Lightning Source LLC
LaVergne TN
LVHW090040080526
838202LV00046B/3899